CRAFT
BREWERS
OF
ONTARIO

CRAFT BREWERS OF ONTARIO

Bill Perrie

WMI
BOOKS

CRAFT BREWERS OF ONTARIO

Published by:
WMI Books Inc.
161 Frederick Street
Toronto, ON M5A4P3

ISBN 0-9736707-6-2

Printed and bound in Canada

CONTENTS

FORWORD

*W*HILE THE CANADIAN BREWING industry predates Confederation by 200 years, writing a book on the craft brewing industry in Canada, and specifically in Ontario, would have been an impossibility only 20 years ago. *Ontario Craft Brewing* is a testament to the passion and drive of Ontario's entrepreneurs who have given life to a craft brewing renaissance.

Ontario craft brewers distinguish themselves by passionately focusing on brewing great tasting beer and creating unique beer experiences. As one brewer says, "if you want to meet the owner, go to the brewhouse and you'll be sure to find him there."

The Ontario Craft Brewers currently boast a portfolio of over 120 hand crafted beers, each with their own distinctive taste and style, but they all share a single passion for crafting great tasting beer. Each craft beer is brewed in small batches, handcrafted by local brew masters using authentic recipes and the finest all natural ingredients. Unsurpassed freshness is the result of small batch brewing, direct delivery to customers and unending attention to quality.

Ontario Craft Brewing explores the chances taken, the success stories in the making, and the sheer variety and vibrancy of the Ontario industry. Each brewery is as unique and different as each individual brew master. Some breweries replicate carefully guarded old European brewing secrets going as far as matching the PH balance in their water to that of Czechoslovakia; while others craft their own signature styles and create new taste experiences by adding chocolate, black cherries, cranberries, ginger and rosemary, and other carefully guarded, mouth watering tastes to their extraordinary beer.

As *Ontario Craft Brewing* explores these small brewers nestled in communities across

Ontario from Carleton Place to Windsor and Niagara Falls to Muskoka, you will discover that each brewery reflects the unique style and personality of its brew master.

Ontario craft brewers are dependant on their local community's support, and are committed to giving back to local communities through job creation, economic development and community involvement.

While today's Craft Brewers occupy a comparatively small portion of the Ontario beer market, there is plenty of room to grow, and growing they are! At the same time, their local roots, small production and distinctive personalities will allow you to discover those one or two new Ontario craft beers that will become your personal favorites!

Bill Perrie has been a friend and long time advocate of the Ontario craft brewing industry. His personal dedication and passion for craft beer will let you explore Ontario's craft brewers through the eyes of a true beer enthusiast who knows each of these breweries and brew masters personally.

Ontario Craft Brewing is a truly great step in recognizing and celebrating Ontario's craft brewing renaissance. I am pleased to introduce this new book and ask you to get involved in creating part of Canada's new brewing heritage. Taste the difference.

Continue your journey with the Ontario Craft Brewers by visiting us at ontariocraftbrewers.ca

Cheers,

John Hay
President
The Ontario Craft Brewers

HISTORY OF BREWING IN ONTARIO

*I*N Ontario we began drinking beer because we were told to.

To stem the flood of American-style Republicanism, stimulate the economy, and slake the British Army's thirst, Upper Canada's Governor John Simcoe, in 1873 arranged for the establishment of a brewery in the hope that wholesome malt liquor would replace ardent spirits as the drink of choice among the lower classes. It would be a most desirable circumstance if this substitute could bring about the general improvement of the morals of the local population by cutting off the consumption of imported American whisky.

The introduction of malt liquors into general use would have other good effects as well. First would be the promotion of husbandry (farming) as opening a market to the farmers to the sale of barley, and secondly by limiting the export of capital used for the purchase of a foreign whisky.

Formosa Spring Brewery, 1885. Opened in 1870, the brewery is still working. PHOTO COURTESY OF GREY-OWEN SOUND MUSEUM

Finkle's tavern brewery and distillery in 1913. Reputed to be Upper Canada's first brewpub. PHOTO FROM THE BOWERING COLLECTION

The brewery Simcoe sanctioned was to be in Niagara-on-the-Lake, and promised to subsidize the local market for barley. No one seemed to immediately take up the Governor's offer, but events would soon lead to the establishment of a brewery simply because of the potential demand. The Loyalist settlers of Upper Canada, consisting of English, Germans, Irish and Scots considered beer a necessity. As the province grew every major European group brought their food, their language and their beer to the new land.

Two breweries vie for the honour of being the first. Tradition favours the Loyalist brothers John and Henry Finkle who are said to have opened a tavern brewery sometime before 1793 near Bath. Their ale, according to artist and traveller William Berczy who tasted it in 1798, was "very good." Another claim is also made for the Bajus Brewery in Kingston which was started sometime in the 1790s to serve the thirsty British garrison.

As much as the pioneers enjoyed their beer, it was the British Army who put the brewing industry on a firm foundation. Because, if the French Army, according to Napoleon, marched with full stomachs, the British marched with full mugs. After 1792, every British soldier was entitled to six pints of small beer per day when billeted with an innkeeper, or five mugs when in barracks. Still not satisfying enough for the lads' palates, the War Office canceled the ration in 1800 and replaced it with "beer money", allowing the boys to buy their favourite tipple.

In one swoop Upper Canada's brewing industry was secured and breweries were established around every garrison. As the headquarters for Imperial forces in Upper Canada, Kingston became the heart of the industry. Within 25 years Kingston alone boasted four breweries serving 136 taverns and 8,000 eager customers. Even the Molson's ventured out of their Montreal stronghold to open a brewery here, making a brown ale that failed to capture the market, sending them back a decade later to Lower Canada.

Beer was a cash product that served a willing spendthrift clientele, and provided the capital needed by Ontario's brewing dynasties in a cash short economy. London's Thomas Carling was persuaded to give-up farming and turn to brewing by the local garrison in 1840 after serving his ale at local building bees. John Labatt followed his example several years later. York (Toronto) became home to numerous breweries and it is no coincidence that Methodist Joseph Bloor opened a brewery in the Rosedale Ravine in 1830, just down the slope from an Army blockhouse.

The Army's thirst was so crucial to the industry that when the 10,000 Imperial Troops were withdrawn from Canada in 1870 beer production slumped, federal excise taxes from beer sales declined and overall consumption fell by five percent.

Beer was the settler's favourite beverage. It was also an ideal pioneer industry as it provided an end product for bulky crops, and as it was made over the winter months its production gave farmers and labourers gainful employment during idle winter months.

It was an essential part the diet as water wasn't always pure due to animal and human contamination. Porter, the Irishmen's favourite, was even recommended by doctors as it contained lactose. The fresh yeast in the bottle also helped digestion. John Fisher of Portsmouth, just west of Kingston, claimed that his beer was "Recommended by most

Bajus Brewery, Kingston. The low building on the left dates to the 1790's while the tower built in 1856 is decorated with a beer barrel and mash tun.
PHOTO FROM THE BOWERING COLLECTION

BLOOR'S BREWERY.

Bloor's Brewery in the Rosedale Ravine, 1830 - 1864. Demolished, 1875. PRINT FROM THE BOWERING COLLECTION

prominent physicians for invalids...natures own tonic." Not only was beer a tonic, it was a cooking ingredient. In 1900, Dow claimed that "...the Best Cooks use Dow's when Ale or Porter is required."

If you were so unfortunate as to live in a locality that did not have a brewery you made your own. Upper Canada's most famous home-brewery is found in Hamilton's Dundurn Castle, the home of Sir Allan McNab, one-time leader of the United Canada.

Today light-coloured and flavoured lagers dominate the mass market, while micro-brewers produce more robust dark ales, lagers and some Belgium beers. Many microbrewers claim to brew traditional beer according to the German Pure Beer Law of 1516 (Reinheitsgebot) that stated only barley malt, water and hops (yeast was added later) could be used to brew beer.

As many of the early Ontario immigrant English and Irish brewers lacked knowledge of the German laws, the beers they produced weren't up to German standards. In fact, if you were to try pioneer beer your palate would receive quite a shock. It was probably dark, almost chewy, sweet, with or without hops and likely full of yeast. At the time of Confederation, Ontario's top ten brews in order were Dark Ale (sweet), Porter (roasty), Pale Ale (hoppy), Amber Ale (balance malt and hops), India Pale Ale (strong and hoppy), Double Stout (strong and sweet), Barley Wine (sweet and strong, 9% or more), Champagne or Brilliant Ale (spritzy) and Mild Beer (un-hoped). Not a single lager or Belgium-style beer on the list.

Without the necessary raw ingredients at hand, brewers made do with maple syrup, treacle and molasses. Some brewers cheated by adding such things as chalk, opium and strychnine (for aging). Even a conscientious brewer such as John Flindall of Trenton recommended the addition of allspice, capsicum, gentian root, quick lime, ice root, pea meal, savoury, Spanish licorice and burnt sugar for brown stout.

John Carling saw the need to improve the local brew through education, while serving as the federal Minister of Agriculture, was instrumental in establishing both the Ontario Agricultural College at Guelph, now Guelph University, and Ottawa's experimental farm. For his efforts he followed the traditional British route from Beerage to Peerage and became Sir John in 1893. Today his legacy can still be found while driving down Ottawa's Carling Avenue.

By the end of the 19th century beer's taste had improved to the point that the Kingston News reported that in some beers at least,

Dundurn Castle overlooking Burlington Bay. Brewhouse with kettle over hearth. Mash tun and underback. restored brewery is next to the kitchen. PHOTOS FROM THE BOWERING COLLECTION

Photo 6 Percy and Evan with their dog Spot prepare to serve the lads a pint or two of their fancy in the Carleton House tap room, Cornwall, circa 1910. Located a day's steamer ride from Montreal, they could enjoy the best from Ontario and Quebec. The line-up included Molson's I.P.A., Dow Ale, Cornwall Ale, and McCarthy's from Prescott.

PHOTO COURTESY CORNWALL MUSEUM

"Only the choicest Bavarian and Canadian hops (likely from Prince Edward County) and best Canadian barley carefully selected by competent judges are used, and in the process of production the full strength and virtue of each constituent is extracted and resolved into a union that has found unusual favour with connoisseurs."

For the first 100 years English ales dominated the market. John Flindall dark, malty ale was like "Mother's milk to an Englishman", while at the other end of the spectrum, John Brain whose family brewed their potent barley wine from 1832 to 1916 said, "Anything under 30% content wouldn't be fit to drink."

Along with brown ales, the English specialized in India Pale Ale. Back then it was a well-hopped beer of not less than 6% alcohol made for the most demanding customer of all, the British army. John Labatt Jr. made his name with India Pale Ale, brewing it to earn his master brewer's degree. Labatt first brewed its IPA in 1865, and it was available until 1993.

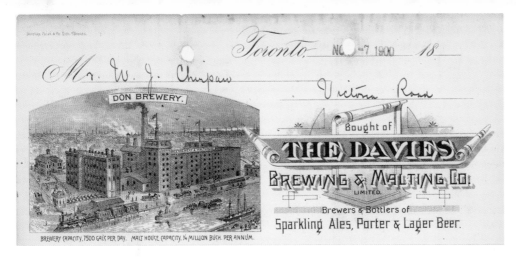

Photo 7 The Don Brewery, Toronto, first started in 1849, gutted by fire in 1907. The brewery entranceway decorated with sculptured clusters of hops can still be seen a 19 River Street. PRINT FROM THE BOWERING COLLECTION

Market demand for clear, sparkling beers led the innovative English and Irish-trained brewers to develop cream, crystal and champagne ales, rather than copy the German-style lagers. The most famous cream ale was first made by John Sleeman. Irishman Henry Calcutt, near Peterborough, brewed a Champagne Ale and Thomas Davies at Toronto's Don Brewery made sparkling ales. The Don Brewery was destroyed by fire in 1907, and apparently not covered by insurance, Davies charlatan-half tried to sell the brewery as a "going concern" to gullible Americans. With no takers by 1910, Davies was being pursued by bill collectors and disconnected his telephone and closed his office.

The Irish and British officers mostly enjoyed a good pint of porter. Irishman. Pat Cosgrave was convinced that all Upper Canada needed to thrive was some good Irish porter. To meet this demand he opened a brewery in 1852 along the banks of the Credit River in the Village of Pucky Huddle - not far from Square One in Mississauga today. Not exactly in the right place at the right time, Cosgrave relocated to Toronto to work first with Eugene O'Keefe. The brewery struggled and was forced to sell bootlegged temperance beer during prohibition to Americans, and was finally acquired by Canadian Breweries in 1936. Cosgrave's partner Eugene O'Keefe from Cork, started his North American career as an accountant, but ended up marrying the brewer's daughter and founded O'Keefe's Breweries.

No Ontario German settlement could be truly called complete without its own brewery. German immigrant breweries opened across Bruce, Grey and Waterloo Counties in Bamburg, Berlin (Kitchener), Carlsruhe,

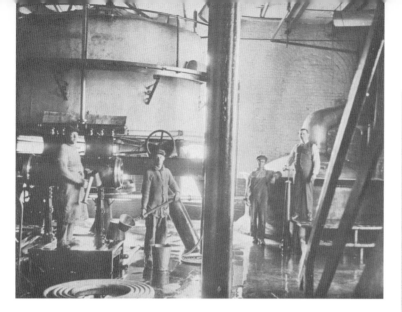

The brewhouse at St. Lawrence Breweries, Cornwall, 1919. Cornwall's Town Council believed the local industrial workforce needed a brew to call their own, and to stimulate local business, Council granted the brewery's investors tax incentives. Sadly prohibition forced the brewery to make near beer to stay in business. The beer did not meet wide acceptance, and the brewery became the first municipally-backed enterprise to close. PHOTO COURTESY CORNWALL MUSEUM

New Hamburg, Owen Sound, Paisley, Walkerton, and Waterloo to name just a few locations. The heritage of these breweries can still be found in Formosa, Neustadt and at Waterloo's Huether Hotel and Lion Brewery where they have been making suds on and off since 1842.

For the beer aficionado, the Germans created the modern beer when George Rebscher of Berlin introduced lager to the Canadian palate sometime after 1840. Up the street David Kuntz founded the Park Brewery in 1844. A local census taker who took his job seriously reported in 1861 that Kuntz's beer was, 'The best in the country. The brewery, Cellars and House are of first quality." The brewery later became part of Canadian Breweries under the Carling label and ended its days as a Labatt's plant.

Lager remained a regional style until Eugene O'Keefe constructed a special lager plant in the late 1870s. Still second to ale, the style did not come to dominate the Canadian market until the lads acquired a taste for the spritzy American lagers during World War II.

The temperance movement, which eventually became prohibition never had much of an impact, and much of Ontario simply ignored it. Central German Ontario, didn't understand it, and it was common for innkeepers to keep two taps: one full of near beer for the inspector and one with beer for the clients.

The temperance movement was imported to Canada from the United States in 1827. British-born Canadians appreciated the temperance crusade for what it was, a New World attack on their institutions and values. In 1833, a correspondent for a Toronto paper, writing in support of honest English ale penned that "...as we value our own peace, let us crush fanaticism, with all, ambitious demagogues (teetotalers), drench all enemies of British immigrants with unmitigated alcohol, and turn seriously to drinking beer."

Retired British Colonel Thomas Talbot thundered that temperance was a Yankee plot, and said that temperance advocates had "commenced their work of darkness under the cover of organizing Damned Cold Water Drinking Societies, where they met at night to communicate their poisonous and seditious schemes."

Supported by such groups as the Women's Christian Temperance Union, the movement grew like a pernicious weed, and scored its first victory with the Dunkin Act of 1864, which allowed for local option.

To fight the "drys", the Canada Brewers and Maltsters Association was founded in 1878. The temperance movement started to lose steam around 1900, largely due to the fact it was failing to stem the public's enjoyment of beer, and encouraged bootlegging in dry counties. World War I gave prohibition new life as the "drys" argued that alcohol production sapped vital resources from the economy and workforce needed for the war effort. With the support of the Minister of Militia and Defence, Sam Hughes, the Ontario Temperance Act was passed on September 1916 while the boys were away in the trenches. For Ontario's 44 breweries the law meant they either had to diversify, close, sell their products by mail order, or produce 2.5% near beer. In December of the same year, Ottawa said that all breweries and distilleries had to close for the duration of the war.

Almost ten years after the war, on June 1, 1927, the Ontario Liquor Control Act became law and breweries could once again begin brewing for home consumption, while hotels were restricted to selling 2.5% beer, sarcastically called "Fergie's Foam," after the dry Conservative Ontario Premier. Our ever-thoughtful legislators at Queen's Park in Toronto met the public's need for beer by authorizing the creation of Brewer's Warehousing Co. Ltd., which evolved into the monopoly known as Brewer's Retail.

After the war, despite the ban on local consumption, many breweries opened to supply beer to the United States, which was now under the Prohibition laws. Ontario brewers might not be able to sell full-strength beer at

Photo 10 Women's Christian Temperance Fountain, Lindsay, 1900. The good women believed that if they offered men clean, pure water they would drink it rather than beer. These fountains designed for man and beast alike were built across Ontario. PHOTO FROM THE BOW-ERING COLLECTION

Select "Table Beer." Brewer's would use nearly any term to avoid saying the product was near beer or non-alcoholic. This pure table beer brewed in Cornwall would have had an alcoholic content of 2.5%. Imbibers claimed you would float away before becoming drunk. LABEL COURTESY CORNWALL MUSEUM

home, but they could make it. Brewers sprang into action and opened plants along the Detroit River at Walkerville, Riverside and Tecumseh. To pay homage to Ontario laws they claimed to be export breweries. Sensing Americans would long for the taste of "Bud", Cosgrave's of Toronto became Canada Bud Brewery in 1926 to sell our own version of the Budweiser brand to thirsty Americans. To quote Ontario Magistrate S. Masson, smuggling booze stateside was an American problem, and "There is no burden cast upon us to enforce the laws of the United States." All a smuggler had to do was purchase duly excised beer, fill out Canada Custom's form B-13, listing the cargo, value and destination of the shipment and boat." If the vessel happened to be a rowboat full of beer headed for Peru from Windsor and returned from Detroit instead an hour later, "nobody asked questions."

American prohibition helped keep some brewers in business, but it was still tough going and by 1930, Ontario's 36 breweries were vying for market share. The industry was ripe for consolidation and E.P. Taylor, with Ottawa's profitable Brading Brewery behind him, acquired Kuntz, Taylor and Bate, British American Brewing and finally Carling to create what soon became Canadian Breweries. Taylor, the ultimate businessman, was intent on rationalizing, consolidating and homogenizing the industry - and the beer it made. In 1954 the conglomerate was scrutinized by the Combines Investigation people to determine if Canadian Breweries was willfully eliminating competition with a monopoly. Despite the fact that Taylor had acquired 23 breweries in 23 years, closed twelve of them, reduced the number of beer brands from150 to nine, and owning a 60% share of the Ontario market, Ontario Chief Justice McRuer did not believe that Canadian Breweries was in a position to overwhelm competition or fix prices.

The writing was on the wall for local brewers - expand or perish. Andrew Peller of Hamilton became the only entrepreneur to open a brewery after World War II. Peller's brewery, today know as Lakeport, was also ultimately acquired by Taylor within six years.

The traditional flavourful, dark ales and lagers brewed by local breweries were history. Pale, sparkling ales, and lagers light on hops and body came with the industry-wide consolidation. Beer was big business and after the war the brewer was a technician, who while he made consistent beer, found himself direct-ed by marketing men, who often gave more creative thought to the label than the beer it advertised. The quintessential '60s lager, Labatt Pilsner Blue was launched in 1951 as a national brand. A sustained advertising campaign, that focused on life-style rather than taste, eventually made it number one. In 1962 standardization peaked when the stubby became the industry's beer bottle.

Molson permanently entered the Ontario market with its Toronto brewery in 1955, and for the next thirty years, Molson, Labatt and Carling-O'Keefe (Canadian Breweries) vied for market dominance. In 1989 Molson acquired Carling-O'Keefe, leaving the market battle to Molson and Labatt. In the late-1980s however, beer lovers' tastes had evolved beyond the bland lagers of the big two. The beer-drinking public wanted a larger choice of European-style beers, and the opportunity for the Ontario microbrewery industry had finally arrived.

In 1984, the Ontario Legislature passed a private-member bill allowing for brewing licenses to be granted to small brewing entrepreneurs, and Jim Brickman was granted the first brewing license in 37 years. Until that time, Molson and Labatt held a vir-tual monopoly in the market, selling 96% of all the beer in Ontario.

Against all odds Brick Brewing became a success, and it has been followed by numerous other microbrewery

Label for Canada Bud, circa 1930. LABEL FROM THE BOWERING COLLECTION

startups. Some have come and gone, but there is now an established, and growing, market for quality beer. The once near-monopoly of Molson and Labatt has shrunk drastically, due in large part to the loyal micro-brew consumers. The best microbrew beers are made by the members of the Ontario Craft Brewer's Association, many of which are in this book. The market for quality microbrewery beers has now been solidly established in Ontario.

Ian Bowering

Beer historian Ian Bowering has written four books about the Canadian brewing industry as well as consulted with numerous breweries about historic beers and has worked on three brewing restorations.

BRICK BREWING Co.

ONTARIO'S FIRST MICROBREWERY OPENED in 1984 and was the brain-child of Jim Brickman, a self-confessed beer lover and one of the most respected men in the brewing industry. Jim's passion for brewing beer began when he spent some time in Switzerland as a young man. Forever the per-fectionist, Jim wanted to learn how to brew beer exactly right, and he later set off visiting breweries around the world, returning from his travels with a wealth of beer-brewing knowledge.

In 1984, Jim opened Brick Brewery in downtown Waterloo. His first beer was a premium pilsner that gave the "imports" a run for their money. His next brew, Red Baron, was another European-style beer and a play on the name of the great German aviator. With a heavy European population in the local area, Jim had immediate success. Never one to sit on his laurels, he then expanded his beer selection to keep up with the times. To date, the Brick Brewery now has eight full-time labels, plus two of Ontario's most famous beers that Brick took over—Connors Best and Formosa Springs Cold Filtered Draught.

Under license, Brick also brews the internationally acclaimed Andech, a product of the Kloster Andech Monastery in the Bavarian Alps, which has a secret recipe over 500 years old. Because of the concern for its freshness and consistency, this beer had never been brewed outside of Germany before. After much deliberation the monks decided that Brick Brewery indeed had the brewing skills to be entrusted with its historic secret recipe.

Jim Brickman: "Behind every brick beer is a brickman."

The brewery has a large retail and beer store, and a hospitality suite aptly named the Red Baron Lounge, which has the look and feel of a cozy local pub. The lounge is famous in Waterloo, and it is here that you will find the annual kick-off breakfast to the Kitchener/Waterloo Oktoberfest festival. It is also famous for Jim's "brewery crawl" beer bottle collection. Many notables have enjoyed a pint or two at the Red Baron, including actor Jack Nicholson and musician Gord Downie. To have the pleasure of a visit and a personal tour, all you have to do is just show up on a Saturday between 12:30 p.m. and 3 p.m. The lounge can also be booked for special events.

In the spring of 2002, Brick brought a Canadian icon back onto the market—the Stubby, a bottle that had not been seen for many years. He filled the Stubby with Red Cap, another great piece of Canadian brewing history and one of the most famous beers of the 1950's and 60's. A piece of marketing genius, the brand and the bottle were welcomed back with open arms.

You can find Brick products all over Ontario in over 400 Beer Stores and over 500 LCBO's, as well as in hundreds of fine bars and restaurants. Jim has been an ambassador for craft brews in Ontario and he was instrumental in helping set up the Ontario Craft Brewers association so that small brewers would have a stronger voice in their ongoing quest to introduce beer drinkers to quality brewed Ontario products. Brick Brewery is a success story and proves that with hard work and dedication—and the ability to change with the times—Ontario beers can succeed in a competitive marketplace.

Brick Brewing Company
181 King Street South, Waterloo, ON N2J 1P7
519 576-9100
www.brickbeer.com

Jim Brickman, Founder and President

TASTING NOTES

Brick Premium Lager

The flagship brand is an all natural malt lager using only 2-row Canadian malt, two types of choice selected European hops, and Formosa spring water to give it a truly distinct European pilsner flavour. It has been a Monde selection gold medal winner numerous times, plus the 2003 winner of best European-style lager in the Canadian Brewing Awards.

Brick Amber

Brick Amber is cognac in colour with a taste that is clean, crisp, and very drinkable. Brewed in small batches without additives or preservatives, Brick Amber is an enjoyable first step into the world of discovering all natural craft beers.

Red Baron

This lighter-tasting Canadian style lager is Brick's most popular brand since its introduction in 1986. Brewed with all natural ingredients like the Premium lager, but with less hop intensity. A Monde selection gold winner.

Waterloo Dark

There is no other beer quite like Waterloo Dark—it is refreshingly light and delicate in taste, but rich in colour. Winner of a Gold Medal for three years running in the Canadian Brewing Awards.

Red Cap

From its peak as one of the most popular beers of the 1950's and 60's, Red Cap is available in the famous "stubby" bottle. It is a smooth ale that is part of Canadian brewing history.

Brick Lager

Brick Lager is an easy drinking beer that is a mildly hopped version of Brick's popular Premium Lager. Brewed with Formosa Springs water, this lager is delightfully refreshing.

Brick Light

Same great taste as the Brick Lager, but with less alcohol content.

Bambay

Bambay is a secluded cove in the Out-Islands of the Bahamas known only to those who can find it. Bambay is a unique citrus-brewed beer, and unbelievably refreshing.

Conners Best Bitter

Centuries ago in Britain, the Ale Connor traveled the countryside examining the worth and measure of each local ale. Connors Best Bitter exceeds those high standards with its robust hop aroma and just right bitter bite. Brewed in the traditional style of an English bitter.

Formosa Springs Cold Filtered Draught

A traditional draught lager with a bright, golden colour and a very drinkable beer for all occasions. Triple Gold Medal winner at the International Monde Selection competition and the Brew Master's medal from the Fine Food and Beverage Federation of America.

Personal Tasting Notes

CAMERON'S BREWING Co.

CAMERON'S IS A GREAT STORY OF A SMALL BREWERY THAT HAD to move to larger premises as demand for its beer picked up. Originally situated in a small facility in Etobicoke, Cameron's opened its doors in 1997 with the launch of Cameron's Cream Ale. This beer was immediately hailed as Toronto's Best New Beer by many beer experts. In the spring of 1998, brew master and president Cameron Howe added the Auburn Ale to his lineup, and again produced a beer that was welcomed by beer lovers, including the internationally acclaimed beer critic Michael Jackson who chose it as the Beer-of-the-Month for his United States-based club. It was with great pride that Cameron's shipped thousands of bottles to eager beer fans in the USA.

The little brewery was getting noticed, and not long after it opened, articles were appearing in the *Toronto Star* praising the Auburn Ale as one of the best they had reviewed. In 1999, Cameron launched his Premium Lager onto the market and this beer also reached the heights of excellence, so much so that it

Cameron Howe, founder and head brewmaster.

captured a bronze medal at the 2002 World Beer Cup—to many the most prestigious beer competition in the world. The popularity of the beers were so great that Cameron made the decision to move to a new 10,000 sq. ft. property in Oakville to help keep up with increased orders. His beers continue to capture awards including gold medals at the Canadian Brewing Awards and the Great Canadian Festival of Beer. Cameron's latest edition to the brewery—Cameron's Dark 266—was unveiled in the summer of 2005 and was voted the best new beer brewed in the Greater Toronto Area at the Golden Taps Awards. The Dark is a chestnut-coloured North American style lager with the complexity of a fine European beer.

With a background in chemical engineering, as well as a passion for home brewing, Cameron followed his love for brewing rather than engineering, and, thankfully for beer lovers, he made the right choice. A serious brewer who believes in the quality and excellence of his product, Cameron is not without humour when it comes to marketing his beers. Indeed, his many slogans, such as "brewed by a connoisseur, not an accountant," are proudly displayed on his beer coasters. The brewery can be toured by appointment, and you will find a good-sized retail and beer store there as well. In addition to the normal 6, 12, and 24 beer cases, Cameron's are available in unique 9, 18, and 27 packs. When asked why a 9-pack, Cameron replied that his motto is "six is not enough."

TASTING NOTES

Cameron's Premium Lager
Pale gold in colour, this award winning lager is a crowd pleaser. Brewed from the finest imported hops and barley, this premium lager was voted one of the best in the world.

Cameron's Cream Ale
This elegant gold ale is crisp and refreshing. Understated hop notes are carefully balanced by a fruity backbone.

Cameron's Auburn Ale
Deliciously complex, the Auburn has a generous hop nose, a long lasting creamy head, and a distinctively smooth finish.

Cameron's Dark 266
Chestnut coloured with a lacy head, Dark 266 combines the deliciousness of a North American style lager with the complexity of a fine European beer.

Cameron beers can be found province-wide at most Beer Stores and LCBO's, and in many fine bars and restaurants, including the famous Victory Cafe on Markham Street and the aptly-named Cameron House on Queen Street West, both in Toronto. The brewery also hosts an annual charity barbecue involving local businesses with all proceeds going to the Oakville Humane Society.

The brewery employs between ten and fifteen people depending on the brewing stages, and only brews small batches to ensure freshness. It will soon be brewing seasonal beers, and you can keep abreast of things by visiting Cameron's website.

Cameron's Brewing Company
1165 Invicta Drive
Oakville, ON L6H 4M1
905-849-8282
www.cameronsbrewing.com

Cameron Howe, President and Head Brew Master.
Jason Ellsmere, Sales and Marketing

PERSONAL TASTING NOTES

CHURCH KEY BREWING Co.

The town of Campbellford is nestled on the banks of the Trent Severn Waterway in picturesque Northumberland County. It is a quaint town with specialty shops and a great little brewery, Church Key, which is situated on the outskirts of the town's limits. Many brewers don't have the luxury of a building or premise to add to the romance and character of their brews, but this is not so in Church Key's case, as it is located in an Methodist Church built in 1878. This charming old building certainly makes the visit to the brewery that much more worthwhile. Founded in 2000, Church Key is the only micro-brewery in the county and a welcome addition to the area. In fact, the brewery has had so much success that in January 2006 they had a celebration to honour the pouring of its one-millionth pint.

John Graham, brewmaster.

Brew master and owner John Graham is a self-taught brewer who started by managing a brew-on-site-store until his considerable skills led him to open his own award-winning brewery. His first brew was the Northumberland Ale, a throwback to the popular tavern ales of the 1940's and 50's. He then went on to create Holy Smoke Scotch Ale, which uses smoked whisky malt direct from Scotland. This ale has received the highest accolades from beer lovers everywhere, and it won gold at the Canadian Brewing Awards two years in a row. In 2004, in conjunction with the city of Peterborough, Church Key brewed Lift Lock Lager to commemorate the 100th anniversary of the Peterborough lift lock. The lager proved to be so popular that Church Key kept it on as a part of their beer family. Church Key is an environmentally-friendly brewery, and, among other things, they have a solar-heated keg washer, an energy-efficient fridge, and delivery vans that run on bio-diesel.

The Church Key retail store is up a flight of creaky steps, and while you enjoy your beer tasting you can marvel in the architecture of the old church or pass the time by checking out John's impressive beer bottle collection. Church Key, like many craft brewers, is a big part of the community, and every May they host a Spring Revival that features local music and food and, of course, plenty of good local beer. Proceeds from the event go to the nearby Campbellford Hospital. This popular event is attended by well over 2000 people.

Church Key beers can be found in many bars and restaurants from Ottawa to Hamilton, in

TASTING NOTES

Northumberland Ale
This Stock Ale was designed to be a throwback to the tavern ales of the 40's and 50's. Crisp light palette with a dry citrus finish.

Holy Smoke Scotch Ale 6.25%
This peat-smoked Scotch Ale is dark and malty, and is enhanced with smoked whisky malt direct from Scotland.

Lift Lock Lager
A refreshing, crisp golden lager, great for all occasions.

Campbellford at the Legion Hall, local golf clubs, and at the one-and-only Stinking Rose Pub. The brewery likes to make craft beers that are distinctive, and this is reflected in Church Key's seasonal brews. In the spring they brew Cranberry Maple Wheat, a beer that uses tart cranberries and fresh local Maple syrup. The summer offering is an ale called Ginger Rosemary Spiced, which is a blend of handcrafted ale and fresh herbs. Finally, in the winter they brew the Decadent Chocolate Porter, a robust ale with plenty of roasted grains and cocoa that comes from the local chocolate factory. John is a great supporter of local business and uses many local ingredients in his beers, as well as selling local honey and bison products at his store. Tours of the church are by appointment, and the retail store is open from 10 a.m. until dark. If it is a nice drive in the country you are looking for, then why not try Nothumberland County and make Church Key your destination? You will be glad you did.

Church-Key Brewing Company
1678 County Road 38
Pethericks Corners, ON
K0L 1L0
705-653-9950
1-877-314-BEER

www.churchkeybrewing.com
John Graham, Brewer and Owner

PERSONAL TASTING NOTES

COOL BEER BREWING CO. INCORPORATED

A BREWING TRADITION SINCE 1997 A.D.

COOL BEER BREWING Co.

*I*N 1997, BOB CRECOUZOS WANTED TO brew a beer that would deserve the name "Cool." It had to be of the highest quality and best ingredients, and have no preservatives, no additives, or chemicals. From the beginning, Cool focused on the brewing process and perfecting their beer. Starting from a tiny brewery in Brampton, the success of the beer grew enough that Cool expanded its operation several times.

In 2003, the brewery launched its new brand, Cool, which soon became a household name in the Brampton area. The same high quality went into their next launch, Millennium Buzz Beer, a hemp-based red lager. The brewery had two of the choicest names in the beer business—Cool and Buzz, the beers were winning awards, including a gold medal at the Canadian Brewing Awards and the Toronto Wine and Cheese Show, and now it was time

Jamie Mistry (center), Brewmaster.

to do the marketing. Go to any beer show in Ontario and you will find the Cool team there, normally lead by super salesman Richard Clemente. The "Cool girls" add style and beauty to any event and are always busy handing out Cool and Buzz merchandise—it is no wonder that the Cool booth is always packed by eager beer enthusiasts! A recent member to the Cool promotional team is well-known radio personality John Bordignon who has brought his endless energy and his savvy ideas to the Cool gang.

The team behind the beer are top notch too, headed up by well-known brew master Jamie Mistry, a BSC graduate of Waterloo University who went on to a post-graduate course in Brewing Distilling Science at the prestigious Herriot Watt University in Edinburgh Scotland. From there Jamie then brewed at the Upper Canada Brewing Co. Also working with Jamie are John Cagliardi, who attended the the Siebel Institute in Chicago, a well-known brewing school, and Shawn Sadler, who worked his way up the

ranks at Cool on his way to becoming a beer expert in his own right.

The brewery has a state-of-the-art keg filling system, which is one of the quickest in the industry. Always innovative, the brewery brought out Cool minis, a seven-ounce version of its flagship lager. This small bottle has become extremely popular for loading into a bucket of ice and enjoying on the back deck, or as a great conversation piece when sharing with friends. Cool beers can be found at most Beer Stores and LCBO's in Ontario, and when in Brampton enjoy a cold pint of Cool or Buzz at several bars including McKenna's, Max's Diner, or Tracks Brew Pub. The Cool brewery has a retail beer store and gift shop as well as home delivery.

The success of this brewery is growing, and

TASTING NOTES

Cool Beer
Cool is a crisp, refreshing blonde lager. It is made with only 100% natural ingredients and cold filtered, with no preservatives or additives. As good as beer gets, and extremely refreshing.

Millennium Buzz Beer
Buzz Beer is a hemp-based red lager made with the finest B.C. hemp, dark roasted Alberta malt and choice German hops. It is cold filtered with no preservatives or additives. This healthy mix of pure, wholesome ingredients, plus the natural goodness of hemp, accounts for its singularly clean, smooth and refreshing taste.

another move is planned in the near future from its present 19,000 sq. ft. premise in Brampton to a new 27,000 sq. ft. building in Etobicoke. Cool beer is a fun company that believes drinking beer should be fun, and this is reflected in their unique marketing strategy. They are, however, very serious about the quality and consistency of their brews. So next time you are at a beer show or festival, make sure to check out the Cool exhibit and say hello to the gang.

Cool Beer Brewing Co. Inc.
54 Bramsteele Road, Unit 20
Brampton, ON L6W 3M6
1-888-844-COOL.
www.coolbeer.com

Bob Crecouzos C.E.O.
Jamie Mistry, Brew Master
Penny Livadaras Brewery Manager
John Bordignon, Marketing

COUNTY DURHAM BREWING Co.

C RAFT BREWERS ARE WELL-KNOWN FOR the passion they have for their work, with long hours spent on everything from brewing, marketing, delivering - and even repairs - to get that final beer into the hands of the drinker. If there is one brewer who fits into the category of a "one-man show", then that would be Bruce Halstead of County Durham Brewing Company. The former computer technician started his new career by dabbling in weekend home brewing with fellow members of the Eastenders Brew Club. It became became more and more time consuming and eventually a full time job.

Bruce began with a location that would handle three different brews in small batches and a few clients here and there, but as the popularity of the beers grew, so did the volume and the number of brands he created.

Bruce and Christina Halstead

The famous C'est What bar in Toronto, a mecca for fine beer drinkers, liked Bruce's beers so much that they commissioned him to brew several of their own in-house brands, including a special cask ale. A great believer in cask ales, County Durham has two great beers available on pump; the Triple X cask and the ESB bitter, which is also available in a nitro keg. With a shelf life of about a week the cask ales are the freshest beers that anyone can enjoy at their local bar. Another popular choice is the County Durham Signature Pale Ale, a beer that is true to the characteristic pale ales of

England. Blak Kat Stout is a nitro-keg stout that appeals to drinkers of both Murphy's and Beamish, as it is somewhere in the middle of these two - more sweet than dry. The brands for the C'est What clientele are indeed speciality brews with the likes of Hemp Ale (which uses Ontario-grown hemp seeds), Coffee Porter, Chocolate Ale, M.B.A. (mild-brown ale), a 6.1% Rye Beer and the in-house favourite, Al's Cask Ale. If you have never been to C'est What then a treat awaits, as you can try all these in-house brands along with many other Canadian craft brews. County Durham's own brands

can also be found also at many other fine bars and restaurants in the area including Smokeless Joe's, Dora Keogh's, The Bow and Arrow, and closer to the brewery, The Waterfront in Pickering.

County Durham Brewing Company is the only brewery in Durham Region and it is well worth a visit to sample some of the great beers. Incidentally, the brewery was not named after its location in Durham Region in Ontario, but rather that Bruce's wife Christina is from County Durham in England, near Newcastle. The symbol on the brewery's logo is a depiction of the doorknob on the cathedral in County Durham.

If you visit, call ahead for opening times, as being a one-man show, Bruce may be out on a delivery. Come bottling time though, Bruce does get some help as its all-hands-on-deck with friends and family volunteering and rolling up their sleeves to pitch in. From the humble beginnings of home brewing, to a small brewery that was originally designed for only three brews, this lover of fine beers certainly has his hands full with ten permanent brands plus a few

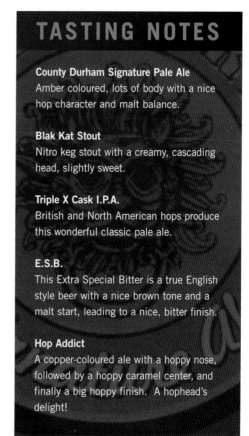

TASTING NOTES

County Durham Signature Pale Ale
Amber coloured, lots of body with a nice hop character and malt balance.

Blak Kat Stout
Nitro keg stout with a creamy, cascading head, slightly sweet.

Triple X Cask I.P.A.
British and North American hops produce this wonderful classic pale ale.

E.S.B.
This Extra Special Bitter is a true English style beer with a nice brown tone and a malt start, leading to a nice, bitter finish.

Hop Addict
A copper-coloured ale with a hoppy nose, followed by a hoppy caramel center, and finally a big hoppy finish. A hophead's delight!

more seasonal brews. Bruce takes it all in his stride working all hours to get the job done and most importantly maintain the consistency of each individual brew.

Is there a more hard working passionate craft brewer out there? Maybe - or then again - maybe not.

County Durham Brewing Company
1885 Clements Road
Pickering
905-686-3022

Bruce Halstead President and Brew Master
Website: www.durhambrewing.com
Email: halstead@Durham.net

PERSONAL TASTING NOTES

GRANITE BREWING Co.

*T*HE GRANITE BREWERY IN UPTOWN TORONTO is one of the best brewpubs you will ever visit, as it has award-winning beers on tap and a great mouth-watering menu that will keep you coming back again and again. The décor of the pub is cozy, and the warm furnishings of the place create a perfect backdrop. The Granite's sister brewpub has been a landmark on the Halifax bar scene since 1985, and it was there that Ron Keefe first learned to brew with his brother before setting off to advance his brewing techniques under well-known brew master Alan Pugsley. In 1991, Ron opened the Granite Brewery in Toronto, and the rest, as they say, is history.

The beers at the Granite are internationally recognized real English-style ales. The Peculiar Strong Ale was given rave reviews by beer critic Michael Jackson, who called it "a classic old ale." Steve Beaumont, a Canadian beer expert, said that the Granite Brewery Dry Hopped Best Bitter had a pronounced fresh aroma reminiscent of a walk in the autumn woods, and gave it high marks. Ian Bowering in his book *In Search of the Perfect Brew* had this to say about the Keefe's Irish Stout: "Keefe's Irish Stout delivers a delightfully complex mouth starting with chocolate malt, followed by roasted malt and cut with light bitterness. Superb."

The Granite has a retail gift shop and a beer store where you can take home these wonderful beers in a variety of styles, including the unique Growler, which at 1.9 litres is almost equivalent to a six-pack. Kegs are also available and start at the 15 litre size all the way up to 58.6 litres. A firkin is also available for cask conditioned ales, and can be rented along with a hand pump or gravity tap. The Indian Pale Ale and the dry-hopped Best Bitter are available in cask. The I.P.A. is one of most traditionally brewed I.P.A.'s you will find in Canada. Tours of the in-house brewery are available only when the brewer is in the building, so one should check ahead before visiting. The restaurant has a large

dining room complete with a central fireplace, and red cherry wood chairs add to the warmth of this lovely room. A canoe that is suspended from the ceiling and makes for a great conversation piece, and don't be surprised to see Laurel and Hardy sitting in their own booth playing chess—these life-size puppets were donated by "The Sons of the Desert," a Laurel and Hardy fan club who meet on a regular basis at the Granite. The front pub area has an inviting library lounge that is perfect for enjoying an ale while reading the newspaper. The pub room also has hardwood floors, and the windows at the front open up to a large street-side patio where you can watch the game on the Granite's big screen TV. A large, covered patio is out back, and it is the perfect spot to enjoy some peace and quiet in this busy area.

The menu at the Granite covers a wide variety of choices—there definitely is something here for everyone. Entrees include dishes such as a Baked Salmon and Shrimp Florentine, Brew Batter Fish and Chips, and a delicious Lamb Curry. The pub has the reputation for having the best baby back ribs in the area, as they are smoked in-house to perfection and go perfectly with Granite's award-winning Stout Drunken BBQ sauce. The brewery has all of its beers on tap as well as a few seasonal favourites, and a full wine

and spirits menu that includes the non-alcoholic Black Granite Root Beer. You can also find great Granite beers on tap in Toronto at C'est What, Café Volo, and the beerbistro. A visit to the Granite will have you hooked—great beers, great food—it is definitely a wonderful brew house.

Granite Brewery
245 Eglinton Avenue East
Toronto, ON M4P 3B7
416-322-0723
www.granitebrewery.ca

Ron Keefe, President
Kevin Keefe, Co-Founder

Ron Keefe behind
Granite's impressive bar

TASTING NOTES

Best Bitter 4.5%
A distinctive copper coloured, full- bodied ale finished with Yakima fuggle hops.

Best Bitter Special 4.5%
Regular bitter, but cask conditioned and dry hopped with wonderful results.

Traditional Indian Pale Ale 5%
Traditionally brewed, light in colour and well hopped. Cask conditioned.

Peculiar 5.6%
Peculiar is a dark ale with a slightly sweet but dry palate.

Ringwood Ale 5%
A filtered pale blonde ale, gently hopped and lightly carbonated.

Ringberry Ale 5%
Ringberry, the first cousin to Ringwood, is a raspberry flavoured blended ale. Very pleasing taste.

Keefe's Irish Stout 4.5%
A black bitter stout with a buried hint of sweetness and a creamy head.

Summer Ale 4%
A special offering, light in colour and alcohol content. It is full bodied and refreshing.

PERSONAL TASTING NOTES

GREAT LAKES BREWING Co.

*A*S YOU DRIVE ALONG THE BUSY Gardiner Expressway in Toronto, you will notice the large sign for the Great Lakes Brewery. Do yourself a favour and pull out of the traffic to visit this well-established local brewery. A large retail area greets you at the front, and of course here you can also sample—and buy—some great, award-winning beers. There is always someone on-hand to talk about brewing with fire-brewed copper kettles. In fact, Great Lakes is one of the very few breweries in Canada that uses the copper kettle brewing method which (of course) was the way all craft brews were made over a hundred years ago. This tradition, and the endeavors of this hard working family, will ensure that beer lovers will always have the great taste of a Great Lakes Brewery product for many years to come.

Peter Bulut Jr., Vice-President

The brother and sister team of Anetta Jewell and Peter Bulut, along with their father, Peter, started the company in 1987 at a 3,500 sq. ft. unit in Brampton. Shortly after they began, their beers were becoming so popular that the family decided to move back to their roots in the Bloor West Village area of Toronto and into a much larger 60,000 sq. ft. facility. Bloor West Village is where Anetta and Peter grew up, and it was only fitting that it should be the home for their expanded brewery.

The first beer to be brewed by Great Lakes was Golden Horseshoe Premium Lager, which has picked up several awards in both the Canadian Brewing Awards and the Great Canadian Brewing Festival. Red Leaf, which took a few years to perfect as Peter

wanted an extra special smooth red lager, picked up the prestigious medal gold at the Great Canadian Brewing Festival and it has received rave reviews ever since. The latest member of the Great Lakes family is Black Jack, a smooth black lager, which is aged longer using four premium malts from the U.K. and Canada.

Anetta believes that the brewery should play a big part of the community, and for years they have supported their local Runnymede Health Centre, holding an annual barbeque for the centre and donating proceeds from their products that are sold at Beer Stores

and LCBO stores on that day to the charity as well. And, if you are a lover of ice cream in addition to beer, then Great Lakes has the product for you. The unique taste of either Red Leaf or Horseshoe lager premium is available in ice cream form. You can take this home in a jar or have a scoop while there.

Great Lakes is located at 30 Queen Elizabeth Boulevard, just slightly west of Toronto. The building is indeed impressive, and tours are available on request. The brewery employs around thirty people, and you can find craft beers from Fort Erie to Ottawa. When looking for a good pint of

TASTING NOTES

Golden Horseshoe Premium Lager
This lager uses fresh hops, Swiss yeast and a blend of three Canadian malts. This full-flavoured lager continues to win gold in the hearts of all who consume it. A testament to the Great Lakes' craft brewing process.

Red Leaf Lager
This is a smooth red lager that has taken years to perfect. Using fresh German hops and special Canadian malts to achieve its colour, this full-flavoured lager contains no additives or preservatives and has received high praise everywhere.

Black Jack Lager
Black Jack is aged longer than most beers with a carefully selected blend of four premium malts from the U.K. and Canada. Perfectly balanced with fresh hops and Swiss yeast, Black Jack is a crisp smooth black lager.

Great Lakes beers try the following places, all of which are in the brewery's vicinity: Mardi Gras, Dr. Generosity, Brydens, and the Rose and Thorne pub. Their beers are also available in many LCBO's and Beer Stores throughout Ontario. The brewery is open for tastings from Monday to Saturday between the hours of 10 a.m. to 6 p.m.

Great Lakes Brewery
30 Queen Elizabeth Blvd.
Toronto, ON M8Z 1L8
416- 255-4510
www.greatlakesbeer.com

Peter Bulut Sr., President
Peter Bulut Jr.,Vice-President
General Manager, Anetta Jewell

PERSONAL TASTING NOTES

HERITAGE BREWING Co.

*C*ARLETON PLACE LIES ON THE OUTSKIRTS OF Ottawa and is a town once renowned for textile and lumber mills and the birthplace of Roy Brown, who is credited with the shooting down of the Red Baron. Today, the old mill buildings are home to condominiums and high-tech industries, but with the banks of the scenic Mississippi River and tree-lined shopping streets, it is a wonderful place to visit, not least because Carleton Place is also home to the Heritage Brewing Company, one of the few breweries in Eastern Ontario, and a godsend to premium craft beer drinkers in the nation's capitol.

Brewmaster Ancil Hartman

The brewery produces a premium lager, a dark lager, and a cask lager, and the much anticipated "Solstice Series"—a collection of seasonal beers that includes a maple beer in the spring, a strawberry in summer, a raspberry rye in the fall (that uses local grown raspberries), and a full blackcurrant lager-style beer in winter. To celebrate Valentine's Day in 2006, Heritage brought out "Passion Brew," a tangy infusion of passion fruit in a lightly hopped lager. All of the seasonal brews are available in 650 ml bottles and kegs, and many restaurants have orders in for these highly-acclaimed beers long before they have even been brewed. Ron's first beer was his Premium Lager, which was originally brewed

in kegs and then bottled as demand rose. He then brought out his Traditional Dark for a writers' festival, and it proved to be so popular that it became a full-time brew.

Heritage brews in small batches every week to ensure their product's freshness, and every step of the brewing process is done using documented procedures to ensure consistency—something that is very important to brewery president Ron Moir. The brewery offers two keg sizes, one being a cask conditioned real lager which comes in a traditional firkin. "With a name like Heritage, what else would you expect?" asks Ron. The beers are packaged in stubby bottles with pry-off tops, and all bot-

tled and kegged beer is double cold-filtered to produce a clear, long-lasting product.

Ron is like a beer politician, but rather than *shake* hands, he wants to put a beer *in* every hand of the people he meets. Heritage beers are available in eastern Ontario Beer Stores and LCBOs, as well as many fine restaurants and bars such as the well-known Highlander in Ottawa and the historic Ironworks in Almonte. You will also find Heritage at many events including those in local art galleries and curling clubs. Heritage does it all—from delivering CO2 and cleaning lines for customers, to "emergency" beer deliveries at all times of the day. The brewery has an on-site retail store

TASTING NOTES

Premium Lager
This carefully crafted premium lager comes from the finest ingredients available. It is bronze in colour, has a full nose, velvety mouth-feel, and a pleasant hop finish.

Traditional Dark
Copper in colour, it has a deep floral nose with nutty malt overtones. It has the colour and hop ratio of the original Bavarian lagers.

where you can pick up standard packs of beer as well as 20-litre and 50-litre kegs.

Carleton Place is just off Highway 7 twenty minutes west of Ottawa. Take a stroll along the banks of the Mississipppi River, do some shopping in the historical downtown, and, most of all, treat yourself to a Heritage lager.

Heritage Brewing Limited
40 Bennet Street
Carleton Place, ON K7C 4J9
613-257-7845
www.heritagebrewing.com

Ron Moir, President
Donna Warner, Sales and Marketing
Ancil Hartman, Brew Master

PERSONAL TASTING NOTES

HOCKLEY VALLEY BREWING Co.

*T*OM SMELLIE, LIKE THE GREAT SIR ISAAC NEWTON, HAD an idea while sitting under an apple tree. Contemplating his future and what he would like to do with his considerable talents, the idea hit him like the proverbial apple—start a brewery! Thus, Hockley Valley brewery was born.

Hockley Valley is a picturesque area just north of Highway 9 and east of Orangeville. The area has winding roads weaving up and down through its green hills and dales. Hockley village is just east of Airport Road, and its quaint little homes and stores make it seem as if it was right out of a Norman Rockwell painting. By the village store you will find the Hockley Valley brewery, complete with its own vintage fire truck parked outside. Indeed, the truck can be seen in many local parades and festivals that are always supported by the brewery.

The brewery is unique as its fine products are only available in cans that are imported from the U.K. The Hockley Dark comes in an English 500 ml can, and the Hockley Gold is in a regular sized 350 ml can, but will soon increase to the English can-size as well. When the brewery idea came about, Tom's first step was

Brewmaster Andrew Kohnen

TRADITIONAL ENGLISH ALE

Hockley
Dark

mild, light body, full flavour

Proudly Craft Brewed in Ontario Canada

www.hockleybeer.ca

500ml

HOCKLEY VALLEY BREWING Co

vol.

to find the right brew master, and he certainly found one of the best in Andrew Kohnen. Andrew had a brewing background going back generations. His family worked in the great breweries of Germany, and after training and gaining certification in England, his first job was in the Gleumes Brewery in Germany. Gleumes was his mother's maiden name, and it was with pride that he worked under the watchful eye of his great uncle's portrait hanging in the brewery. Andrew relished in the fact that he was using the same equipment and

The Hockley girls at the bottling (canning) line.

beer cellar that his distinguished ancestors had also used.

With Tom's English brewing background complimenting Andrew's German one, they found the perfect chemistry to brew both an English-style ale and a German-style ale. The success of both brews have the company moving to a larger premises soon. Not wanting to leave Hockley Valley, they are moving to an old local fire hall, which will be the perfect place for Tom to house his truck. Tom's hard work earned the brewery a Business Excellence Award in 2005, and both brews have received rave reviews and have won top honours in the Canadian Brewing Awards in recent years. The dark beer has a subtle chocolate-roast finish and is made in small batches using imported English malts and hops. The gold beer is a lightly carbonated, blonde-style ale with a crisp, refreshing taste. Part of the success of the brewery is the fact that it uses crystal-clear water from its own well—another reason Tom won't leave the valley, as Hockley sits on a vast underground lake.

TASTING NOTES

Hockley Dark

A deep chestnut-hued traditional English ale with hints of warm caramel, nuts, and a subtle chocolate roast finish. Made with the finest imported English malts and traditional hops.

Hockley Gold

A light-bodied, pale blonde draught-style ale. Lightly carbonated, it rewards the palate with hints of sweet malt, tart hops, and a crisp, clean finish.

There is an old-world style of doing things at Hockley Valley Brewing. Everything is done by hand, even the canning process. Tom believes that the hands-on approach, the small batches, and the slow-brewing process shows up in the finished product. The brewery has five full-time employees and another four who work part-time, though this may change as the demand grows and the production starts at the new premises. It is certainly worth the drive to this scenic area to enjoy a pint of Hockley draught at the nearby Hockley Valley Resort, or in Tottenham at the Village Pizza. Of course, one can always sample at the quaint little brewery—just look for the fire truck, or a figure sitting under an apple tree contemplating his next move.

Hockley Valley Brewing Company
994227 Mono-Adjala Townline
Hockley Village, ON
L9W 2Z2
519-941-8887
www.hockleybeer.ca

Tom Smellie, President.
Andrew Kohnen, Brew Master
Chris Wildman, General Manager

PERSONAL TASTING NOTES

KING BREWERY

*W*hile working under the hood of yet another car at his father's service station, mechanic Phil DiFonzo's thoughts would often wander away from spark plugs and carburetors toward the latest batch of home brew he was making. He was getting quite good at making a quality home beer—so good that he had won several first-place prizes in various home brew association competitions. A fellow mechanic who hailed from a beer Mecca in Bavaria had introduced Phil to the premium quality beers his father had been sending him from Germany. Since Phil enjoyed the beer so much, and since most of these beers were unavailable in Ontario, he decided to make his own. After a few false starts—and much studying and tinkering trying to perfect the brewing art—Phil's work seemed to be paying off. As more and more awards started to come his way, it was

Founder and brewmaster Phil DiFonzo

his brother, Chris, who encouraged Phil to start his own brewery. It was a huge step up from brewing at home, but both men believed in Phil's dedication to the fine art of premium brewing. Chris was a marketing guru so it made sense that he would become Phil's business partner. King is now truly a family business with Phil's daughter, Christina, running the retail side as well as dealing with key accounts. She also shares her father's passion for the business and is relentless in her quest to make King the number one draught in the area.

Phil decided to become a certified beer judge in order to gain a more full understanding of how beers should really taste, and he decided on a Czech-style pilsner for his flagship brew. Forever the perfectionist, he brought in high-quality German decoction-style brewing equipment (which is instrumental in brewing high-class European lagers). He wanted nothing but the best to ensure the authenticity of his brew, and even the ingredients, including Pilsner malt, Saaz hops, and a true Czechoslovakian yeast strain, were all imported, and he decided to use only distilled water to maintain the taste-consistency of his product.

Canadian beer expert Stephen Beaumont told Phil that a quality Ontario-brewed,

Czech-style pilsner was long overdue, but Phil wondered if his beer would it stand up to the high expectations created by brands such as Pilsner Urquel. A little apprehensive, Phil sent Stephen his product to be tasted. He need not have worried, as Beaumont rated it very highly, and it was Stephen who was later instrumental in bringing in Phil's first customer—the Bier Market on Toronto's Esplanade. It was a happy day at the small brewery when the first kegs left the building, bound for the city. From then on, King brewery has not looked back and this true-to-style pilsner has gone on to win many awards, including a gold medal for a European-style pilsner three years in a row at the Canadian Brewing Awards.

King's next beer was a dark lager in the German Dunkel style, and early in 2004 the first deliveries were made to King's key accounts, garnering plenty of positive feedback. This beer won bronze in its first attempt at the Canadian Brewing Awards, and has created a friendly "war of words" at local bars as to which is the best King beer. The King pilsner continues to get rave reviews, and John Filson of the Toronto Star rates it as one of Canada's best.

King Brewery is located in near the village of Nobleton, just east of highway 27 on the

King Road. The brewery store is open Monday to Friday from 10 a.m. to 6 p.m., and again on Saturday between 10 a.m. and 5 p.m. It has a gift shop and a tasting bar. Intimate tours are available by appointment with a guarantee of plenty of "beer chat." Keep checking in with the guys at King as there are plans in the works for world-class seasonal beers.

King Brewery
5645 King Road
Nobleton, ON L0G 1N0
905-859-5464
www.kingbrewery.ca

Phil DiFonzo, President and Brew master
Chris DiFonzo, Vice-President
Mike MacNeal, Assistant Brew master
Christina DiFonzo, Retail Store Manager and Accounts Manager.

TASTING NOTES

King Ultra Premium Pilsner
True to style in every regard, this Czech-style pilsner is brewed with only the finest imported ingredients and distilled water, designed to deliver authentic taste every time. This bright golden, full-bodied, refreshingly great tasting beer has a delicious balance of malt and hops, with a hint of bitterness, making King Brewery Pilsner truly unique in North America.

King Dark Lager
King Brewery's newest addition is the authentic Munich-Dunkel style dark lager. Only the finest imported dark Munich malt and noble German hops give this beer King's trademark "true style" aroma and flavour. This deliciously refreshing red-brown beer is rich and full, delivering a clean bready-taste with a hint of roasted chocolate. Complex yet clean, and extremely flavourful.

PERSONAL TASTING NOTES

LAKES OF MUSKOKA COTTAGE BREWERY

*T*he Muskoka region, with its lakes, granite outcrops, forests full of wildlife, and the smell of fresh air, always leaves you with a hearty appetite—not to mention a hot summer thirst. Cottage country is where thousands of people head every year during all seasons. Whether it is boating or swimming in the summer, or sledding and ice fishing in the winter, Muskoka draws people with its natural beauty. Now there is an even better reason to visit this pristine area—the Lakes of Muskoka Brewery. Situated in Bracebridge, this wonderful cottage brewery has just the right beers to accompany your stay. Brewery founder Gary McMullen traveled the world when he was an aerospace engineer for the military, but his heart always belonged in Muskoka, as it was there that he had his roots and his sense of community.

Already an established home brewer, Gary had the notion of starting his own small brewery, so in 1994, he, along with his business partner, Kirk, opened Lakes of Muskoka Cottage Brewery. While Gary looked after the operation at the brewery, Kirk made sales calls as far away as Toronto, driving there with kegs and samples in the back of an old two-door Dodge Charger. Tough times, but they both passionately believed in what they were doing and carried on. Sadly, Kirk was involved in a car accident later that first year and passed away from his injuries a few months later. Gary now believes that Kirk's spirit is with him at the brewery, and this has given him the strength to tackle any obstacles that come his way throughout the tough world of craft brewing.

The brewery sits in an historical building which was once a feed mill and is now over one hundred years old, and the retail store and gift shop at the front of the building is in a space previously occupied by the town butcher. The brewing process and equipment at Lakes of Muskoka has to be seen to be believed, and it fills up every square inch of Gary's 7200 sq. ft. space—it's a marvel of engineering expertise. In the summer months the brewery operates at full capacity to keep up with the high volume demanded by local bars and restaurants pouring for all of the summer cottagers. But the good news for people who don't travel to Muskoka is that the fine crafted brews of this brewery can be found all over Ontario at select beer and liquor stores. Lakes of Muskoka plays a big part in the community and sponsors the annual Antique and Classic Boat Show, which attracts thousands of visitors.

The brewery's signature beer is Muskoka Cream Ale, and well-known beer writer Jamie MacKinnon gave it four stars in *The Great Lakes Beer Guide* calling it "a great, food friendly beer." Many agree with him,

and the beer has won numerous awards including two gold medals at the Great Canadian Brewing Festival. Gary's other beers have also received high acclaim as well, and the brewery proudly displays all of their awards and accolades.

A visit to the brewery is like stepping back in time. The gift store has many local artifacts and sells many great gifts for home and the cottage. The feed mill has not changed much in appearance over the years and it adds to the charm of this wonderful little brewery.

Lakes of Muskoka Cottage Brewery is well worth a stop on your travels up north, and even better if you can catch one of the tours that take place every Friday and Saturday. You can also try their premium brews at many fine bars such as the Old Station Restaurant, the Inn at the Falls, the Griffin in Bracebridge, the Windermere House in Windermere, Taps in Port Carling, and On the Docks in downtown Huntsville. As the brewery website states, " The only way to improve on Muskoka...was to brew a beer in it"—and that is certainly what they have achieved.

Muskoka brewing team, (from left) Andrew Henry, Alex Maddock and Naresh Harriman

Lakes of Muskoka Cottage Brewery

13 Taylor Road
Bracebridge, ON
P1L 1S6
705-646-1266
www.muskokabrewery.com

Gary McMullen, President

TASTING NOTES

Muskoka Cream Ale
Crisp, refreshingly hopped with a nutty malt finish.

Muskoka Premium Lager
Superbly balanced with a fresh, easy-going body that comes with long aging. A favourite with premium palates.

Muskoka Honey Brown Lager
Made with real honey that adds a delicate floral touch. Mellow and meticulously brewed.

Muskoka Premium Dark Ale
A big ale, rich and flush with hints of coffee, molasses, and finishing with a hint of cashew.

PERSONAL TASTING NOTES

MILL STREET BREWERY

*T*he Mill Street Brewery is in the historic distillery district of Toronto. The area is like the backdrop to a Dickens novel, with cobblestone streets and wonderful Victorian red-brick buildings. It was here that Gooderham& Worts Inc. operated over 100 years ago, distilling rye whisky and rum. The area is now a tourist attraction with trendy shops and boutiques, many fine restaurants, and of course the Mill Street Brewery. When visiting the brewery you half-expect to see Clydesdale horses backing up a cart to be loaded up for beer delivery.

Michael Duggan, Mill Street's president, is a microbiologist and astrophysicist with a wealth of experience in the beer business. Before university, Michael worked for a spell with Coca Cola, and this gave him his first insight into beverage packaging and mar-

keting. While in university he worked for the old Connors Brewery doing a variety of odd jobs, and it was there that he developed his passion for brewing. Michael went on to work as a consultant for many large breweries in Cuba and, in fact, he was instrumental in bringing draught beer to the country. With his two friends, Steve Abrams and Jeff Cooper, Michael returned to Canada with his unique knowledge and experience to open up the Mill Street Brewery in 2002. The 6000 sq. ft. building is an open-concept design with 18 foot ceilings and four enormous skylights. The brewery has been an instant hit in the Toronto area, winning the best microbrewery award in the Greater Toronto Area at the Golden Tap Awards. Mill Street brews can now to be found in bars and restaurants all over the city.

With Michael's background, it is no wonder that the first beer offered by Mill Street was Ontario's first-ever 100% original organic lager, which contains no pesticides, insecticides, herbicides, or chemical fertilizers. This specialty beer is 4.2% alcohol and is brewed using imported organic New Zealand Hallertau hops and Breiss organics 2-row brewers malt—a refreshing beer that not only tastes good, but does you good too! The latest offering from the brewery is Mill Street Coffee Porter, using beans roasted by Mill Street's neighbour, Balzac's Coffee. The beer is truly unique in taste with an intense coffee flavour and a hint of chocolate; so good, in fact, that it won gold at the 2005 Canadian Brewing Awards in the competitive Porter category. Mill Street's Tankhouse Ale also picked up gold in the Pale Ale category during the same year.

The other full-time brew is the Mill Street Stock Ale, which is a golden blonde ale that is crisp, refreshing, and sparkling. Over the Christmas period, the brewery makes its own Barley Wine, which is available by the bottle or in a unique gift pack. The Barley wine is 11% alcohol and is reminiscent of the great barley wines brewed in the United Kingdom over the years. They also brew seasonal beers, including Helles Bock, a strong German lager that is 6.5% alcohol and brewed with 100% organic malt and hops.

Mill Street brews have proven to be so popular that they are having to expand to a new 20,000 sq. ft. facility in order to keep up with demand, but they plan to transform the

Brewmaster Michael Duggan

wonderful building they are currently in into a brewpub and restaurant to further the appeal of the brewery in this historical district. Tours of the brewery for parties of ten or more can be booked by calling Mill Street, or one can join the regular Saturday and Sunday tours that start at 3 p.m. Mill Street also has a sample bar, along with a retail store with many unique gifts for sale.

Mill Street Brewery
55 Mill Street, Building 63
Toronto, ON M5A 3C4
416-681-0338
www.millstreetbrewery.com

Michael Duggan, President and Brew master
Steve Abrams, Marketing Director
Jeffrey Cooper, Sales Manager

FERMENTATIO
VESSEL

TASTING NOTES

Mill Street Original Organic Lager

This 100% all-natural, certified Organic Lager is Ontario's first organic lager and contains no pesticides, insecticides, herbicides, or chemical fertilizers. Brewed with imported malts and hops, this European style pilsner offers a light, crisp, and refreshing flavour with a clean finish.

Mill Street Tankhouse Ale

Like traditional Pale Ales, Tankhouse Ale has a deep copper-red colour, using five different malts to produce a complex malty-texture. The spicy cascades hop is used to give an assertive hop flavour, aroma, and bitterness to the ale. The result is a satisfying and complex tasting beer.

Mill Street Stock Ale

A golden export-style ale made from only malt and hops with no fillers or adjuncts. A brilliant golden colour gives a "sparkling" appearance as the gas escapes from the glass. The natural sweetness of the malt is perfectly balanced by the bitterness derived from the hops. This beer represents the way blonde ales were made 100 years ago.

Mill Street Coffee Porter

The Porter is rich and robust, dark brown in colour, with a dark roasted coffee nose, imparting an intense coffee flavour with notes of chocolate. Made by beans supplied by the Distillery districts Balzac's Coffee, this Porter offers a rich, full, and unique flavour. One of a kind in the current Ontario market.

NEUSTADT SPRINGS BREWERY

*A*s you drive into Neustadt, a sign proudly proclaims that this is one of the prettiest villages in Ontario. Now, there are a lot of pretty villages in Ontario, but there is no brewery like Neustadt Springs, which is located in a beautiful building with as much character and history as you will find anywhere in the province. This grand old brewery was established in 1859, and is reputed to be the oldest operating brewery building in Ontario. It was founded by Henry Huether, a German immigrant who brought over 40 stonemasons to the village to build the brewery. The brewery is situated over natural springs that still flow through the network of caverns carved out of the rock in the brewery's sub cellars. The brewery stayed open until 1916 and then closed due to a decline in population and the prohibition. Lying dormant for 81 years, Andrew and

Val Stimpson, both from the U.K., finally re-opened this historic brewery a few weeks before Christmas in 1997.

Andrew and Val had plenty of experience in the brewing business. They first worked with Daniel Thwaites of Blackburn, England, and then later with the prestigious Border Breweries of Wrexham in Wales. Andrew and Val had operated their own pubs in North Wales, so all aspects of brewing—from the beer's creation to its consumption—was second hand to them. After a holiday in Canada with friends in 1990, the Stimpsons returned the next year to tour more of the country. They fell in love with Canada and wanted to stay, with the idea of staying in the hospitality business. Andrew had thought about opening a pub, but he realized he could not find a Canadian beer he truly liked, so this led him to start thinking about brewing his own beer. The search was then on for a suitable spot, and after two years he found the "perfect" place —the old brewery in Neustadt. It needed a lot of work, but Andrew and Val both saw the immense potential of the building. After an exhausting ten months of renovations, the work finally paid off when villagers lined up to taste the first batch of beer. Selling out in just five hours, Andrew had to go to the local beer store himself to pick up his own beer for his

Christmas Eve drink. The Stimpsons have become a bit of a legend in the Bruce Peninsula, with stories of Andrew driving at all hours of the night to deliver beer to a pub that has run out. He will also take the time to help with draught installations, repairs, and whatever else his clients may need.

Neustadt started off with an authentic Scottish ale, and then a Belgian style lager. The brewery proved to be such a good tourist draw for Bruce County that the local authorities partnered with the Stimpsons to brew Bruce County Premium, a crisp refreshing North American-style lager. The next beer for the brewery was the uniquely named 10W30, which has since become so successful that it has even surprised Andrew. The beer won a silver medal at the prestigious Beer World Cup, and then another silver medal at the Canadian Brewing Awards. The beer has also been adopted by the Canadian MG car club as their official beer of choice. Bruce County Premium lager also won gold at the Canadian Brewing Awards, and Andrew believes that this is because they use wonderful pure spring water, and only the finest aroma and bittering hops from New Zealand and England for their brews.

A visit to the brewery is a must, and a tour of the caverns is truly an experience. Val is a

wonderful host and her tour is augmented by her terrific, dry British humour. The brewery has a retail gift and tasting area, and also serves as a tourist information centre for visitors to the Bruce Peninsula. The village is picturesque, and a stroll around town, followed by a visit to the brewery is a great day out. Neustadt is one hour north of Guelph, two hours north of London, and three hours northwest of Toronto. The Bruce Peninsula is fast becoming a popular tourist destination, and in this area you will find many great pubs who sell the award winning Neustadt products—the Big Tub, the Crowsnest, and the Tub House Pub in Tobermory; Mad Reef Tavern in Port Albert; the Elk and Finch in Southampton; and the well-known Ted's Range Road Diner in Meaford.

Andrew and Val Stimson, the
heart and sour of Neustadt

Neustadt Springs Brewery
456 Jacob Street
Neustadt, ON
519-799-5790
www.neustadtsprings.com

Val Stimpson, President
Andrew Stimpson, Brewmaster
Vickie, Jack of All Trades

TASTING NOTES

Neustadt Scottish Ale 4.5%
Brewed in the traditional Scottish style, deep
golden in colour, full flavoured, smooth, and
with plenty of body.

Neustadt Lager 5%
Full flavoured Belgian style lager which is
smoother than other European style pilsners.
Smooth and creamy.

Neustadt 10W30 5.5%
A traditional dark English Mild—malty but
nice and smooth.

Bruce County Premium Lager 4.5%
A light flavoured beer. Pale golden in colour,
smooth, with plenty of taste.
Perfect Summer refresher.

PERSONAL TASTING NOTES

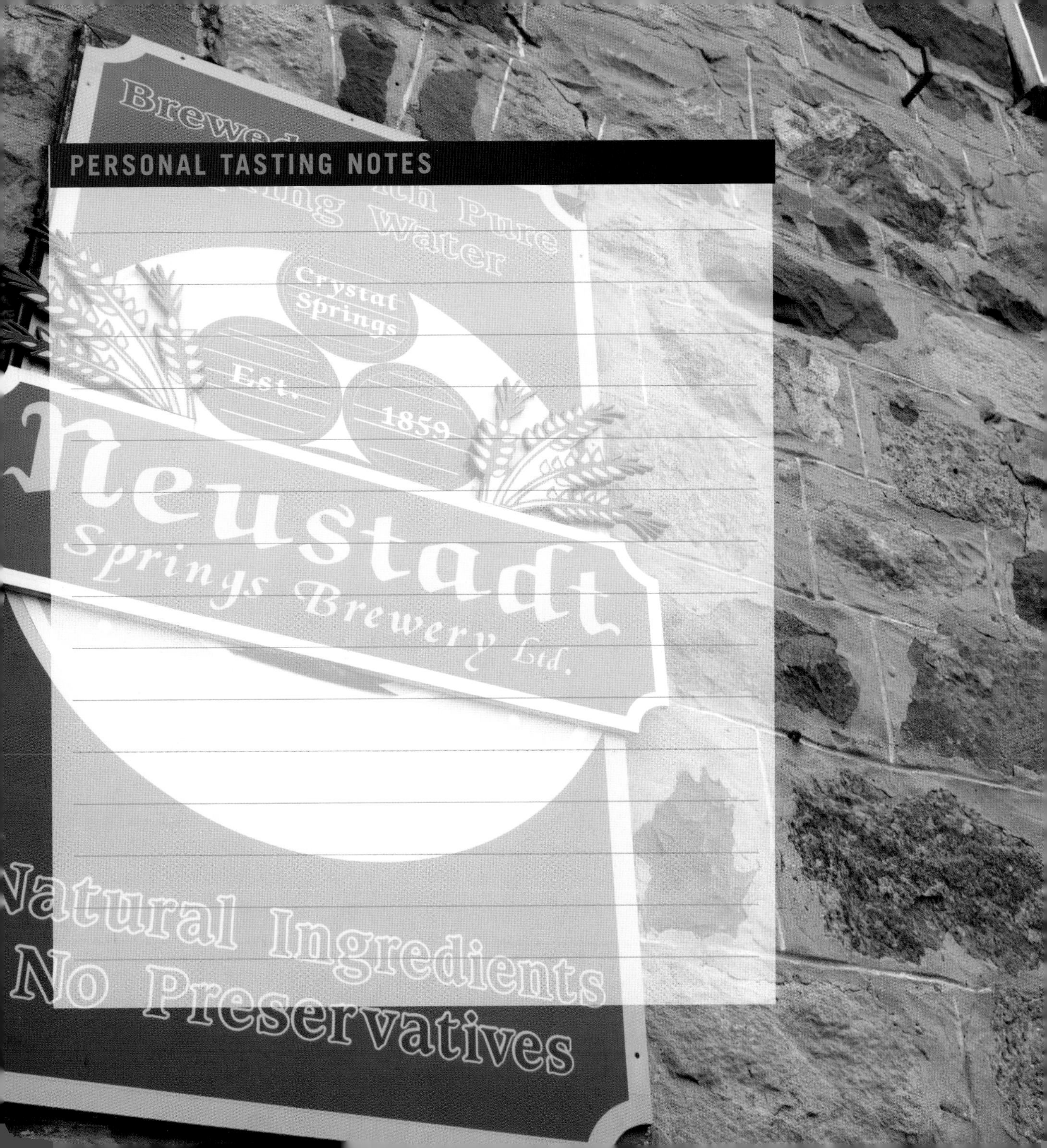

NIAGARA'S BEST BEER

A few years ago, Niagara's best blonde would conjure up visions of Marilyn Monroe in the 1953 thriller *Niagara* where her character, Rose Loomis, plots to murder her husband while on honeymoon in the Falls.

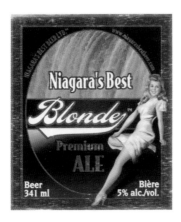

Nowadays, Niagara's Best Blonde is a premium blonde ale brewed in St. Catharines by Niagara's Best Beer Limited.

Kent Kraemer was looking for a family business when an opportunity—in the form of a vacant brewery—appeared. As he had already spent many years with Labatt Breweries in sales and marketing, and his wife, Kristy, also had worked for the company, deciding to open a brewery was an easy choice. After months of cleaning and preparation, their brewery finally opened for business in May of 2005. The decision to brew a blonde ale was calculated one, as it would be the only craft-brewed blonde ale in Ontario; It was a decision that paid off as the beer has quickly gained a loyal following.

Brewer Ken Wieler learned his trade at the award-winning Bushwakker Brewery in Regina, Saskatchewan. A man of many talents, he also holds a degree from Brock University in wine making. The Niagara brewery has state-of-the-art equipment, and is situated in what was once a landmark bakery building in downtown St. Catharines. The brewery has a spacious brick interior, a large tasting bar, and a retail gift store. Plenty of shops and restaurants are located nearby, as well as the local farmers market. Niagara Falls is twenty minutes down the road, and there you can enjoy the taste of Niagara's Best Blonde at both the Fallsview and Niagara casinos. Local St. Catharines bars who feature the blonde ale include Patrick Sheehan's, Pow Wow's, and the Merchant Alehouse.

Tourist merchandise sells very well at the brewery, and this is no surprise since the logo for the beer is the striking figure of a 1940's

Hollywood starlet. Kent and Kristy worked with the prestigious company Courtois and Mather to develop the logo and the rest of the brand's identity. In the end, they nailed the perfect image for the company, and tee-shirts with slogans such as "Everyone's Going Blonde," are doing great business.

The beer itself appeals to a wide range of tastes. Whether you are a lager or ale drinker, the premium blonde ale, with its subtle caramel malt flavour, is popular with drinkers of both styles. Brewery tours are available in the historic building by prior arrangement. Being in the heart of wine country does not phase Kent. " Let's face it," he says, "there's going to be some guy on a wine tour who'd like a nice beer along the way." And a nice beer it is, too.

TASTING NOTES

Niagara's Best Blonde

The full body and clean finish is achieved using a blend of the finest Canadian barley, imported caramel malts, and a touch of toasted wheat. The subtle malt flavour is perfectly balanced by the taste and aroma of North American and European hops.

Niagara's Best Beer Limited
75 St. Paul Street,
St Catharines, ON L2R 3M3
905-684-5998
www.niagarasbestbeer.com

Kent Kraemer, Owner and President
Kristy Kraemer, Owner and Vice President

CONFEDERATION ALE
ROBERT SIMPSON
BREWING COMPANY
CONFEDERATION ALE
ROBERT SIMPSON

The ROBERT SIMPSON BREWING Co.

*I*N 1836, ROBERT SIMPSON, RENOWNED brew master and the first mayor of Barrie, built Simpson's Brewery in the small village of Kempenfelt on the shores of Lake Simcoe. A year or so later the building was destroyed by fire. Robert Simpson then moved his operation to the south shore town of Tollendal and again the brewery was destroyed by fire a few years later. Finally he moved to the foot of Mary Street by the lake in the soon-to-be boomtown of Barrie. Using traditional steam kettles his brews were to become a big part of Barrie's early brewing history.

President and founder of today's brewery Peter Chiodo saw amazing potential for a craft brewery to once again grace the shores of Lake Simcoe, and in honour of Barrie's

first mayor and the wonderful heritage of his beers, Peter decided to resurrect the proud name and tradition that was the Robert Simpson Brewery.

Forever the perfectionist Peter did not do things lightly and it took five years of planning before the "little brewery on the lake" opened its doors.

The building is a credit to the downtown core of Barrie with the elegant front of the brewery fitting right in on the main shopping street (Dunlop). The back of the brew-ery faces onto Lake Simcoe and is indeed only a few hundred yards from where the original Simpson brewery stood. Everything about this brewery is class, from the retail gift store at the front where only top of the line merchandise is to the upstairs event room with its central fireplace and elegant furnishings. Even the packaging of the beer is second to none with the six and twelve pack cases winning gold medals at the prestigious PAC awards for brand marketing. The actual bottle label also won a gold medal for labels with its innovative use of thermo chromatic ink, an actual thermometer on the label lets you know and displays the correct temperature to thoroughly enjoy your beer.

Obviously a brewery has to be known for its beer in addition to its packaging and it is here that Peter exceeded even his own high expectations. The brewery enticed renown Brew master Gordon Slater out of retirement on certain conditions that Gord requested, such as a state of the art laboratory so that he had the resources at hand to make certain that the beer maintained its consistency. Gord has a degree in microbiology obtained from Guelph University and top honours from Wisconsin University brewing school along with the completion of packaging school in Michigan State, his advanced microbiology studies continued at Colorado State University. Gord is a great believer in craft brewers and has lobbied the government in the past to support the smaller brewer. When it comes to brewing Gord has done it all from being a microbiologist at Molson to head brew master at several craft breweries.

The brewery then needed a top-notch salesman and marketing director and again they hired one of the best when they secured the employment of Terry Zuk. Terry has over twenty-five in the beer industry. Terry brings enthusiasm and incredible knowledge to Robert Simpson Brewery.

The pieces were beginning to fit for the Robert Simpson team. In 2005 the brewery won Gold at the Canadian Brewing Awards as their premium Confederation Ale picked up "Best in the Cream Ale Category" a category that saw a record amount of entries that year. The brewery has a mini brewery on site where every employee gets to learn the art of brewing to better understand the whole process. The brewery also has a beer apprenticeship and beer school program along with excellent tours of the building, check out the website or call the brewery for details.

You can also enjoy a pint of Confederation Ale in most bars and restaurants in the Barrie area and in many Beer and liquor stores. Make sure you pay a visit to the 'little brewery by the lake" in Barrie. You will be glad you did.

The Robert Simpson Brewing Company.
107 Dunlop Street East, Barrie, L4M 1A6
705-721-8989

Peter Chiodo Jr. President.
Gordon Slater. Brew master
Wally Rudnisky Director
Terry Zuk V.P. Sales and Marketing

tony@robertsimpsonbrewery.com
www.robertsimpsonbrewery.com

Brewmaster Gordon Slater

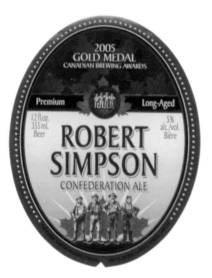

TASTING NOTES

Confederation Ale

Using only the finest ingredients including seven select grains of malted barley, specialty hops, premium yeast and the purest water from their own spring. A distinctive process of cold fermenting and long aging results in a harmonious golden ale with just the perfect patina. A subtle Saaz hop aroma presents very light floral and citrus notes with a unique undercurrent of sweet clover to round the bouquet off. A none too fleeting malty sweetness introduces the beer, which slides into a complex yet delicate body with a slightly dry mouth feel and smooth hop finish.

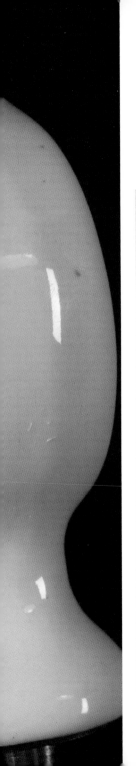

TRAFALGAR BREWING Co.

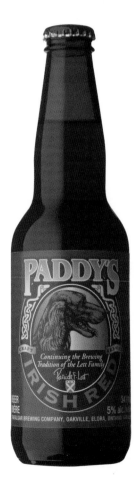

O ne of the few breweries to have its own pub, Trafalgar Ales and Meads—originally known as the Trafalgar Brewing Company—is a place where one can visit and enjoy the tastes of the many fine brews in the cozy Tied House Pub. There is always a great selection of Trafalgar brews on tap, and a menu that will keep bringing you back.

The company was founded in 1993 by Mike and Nancy Arnold along with George Hengstman. From its small beginnings, the company has grown into one of the most progressive of small breweries. The brewery experiments with new brews in its unique one-hectolitre pilot plant. Their experimentation has resulted in an amazing array of fine products, including an impressive line up of meads (a mixture of honey, fruit juice, and malt). Head brew master Dave Jamieson has a wealth of brewing experience and a background in chemical engineering. Dave enjoys the challenges of keeping so many fine brews consistent, and he has a fine team of brewery personnel to back him up. According to the law, all tanks in the brew house have to be individually identified. Most breweries use a numbering system, but Trafalgar instead gives the tanks names. The fermentation and ageing tanks are named after women (due to the nurturing nature of women), and the bright tanks are named after

men (who are always under pressure). The exception to this is the mead tanks, which are named after excise officers who have visited the brewery.

It's difficult to summarize Trafalgar, as they have nine full-time beers, three seasonal beers, and six different meads. All of these beverages are premium craft brewed, and the brewery has picked up countless awards over the years, including a gold at the prestigious World Beer Championships.

One of the most intriguing brews is the Celtic Brown Ale, which is based on an ancient recipe for Irish brown ale. This fine beer is also the base for the great chicken wing sauce available in the pub. The meads are available in many fruit flavours, including raspberry, black currant, and an exotic tropical mix of pineapple, orange, and mango. The meads are 9% alcohol, and are somewhat like a fruit-flavoured champagne.

Dining at the pub is a great way to relax and enjoy some great beer-based dishes such as the Trafalgar clubhouse, which is a triple-decker sandwich with sliced chicken, peameal bacon, cheese, lettuce, and tomato on toasted beer bread. The Portside beef dip is a house favourite, with tender slices of roast beef marinated in Trafalgar's Portside Amber Ale, and topped with onions and Swiss cheese on toasted beer bread. The bar staff are extremely knowledgeable about the beers available, and certainly make the visit that much more interesting with an insightful background into each brew. The pub is open Tuesday to Saturday from 11 a.m. to 10 p.m, and Sunday from noon to 4 p.m. The retail beer store is open seven days a week. If you would like a tour of the brewery, ask any of the staff at the pub or the retail store to book one for you.

Trafalgar beers and meads are available throughout Ontario and at most Beer Stores and LCBO's. The brewery is located in Oakville, just south of the Q.E.W. The brewery is a great place to pop by and grab a bite to eat while learning more about the wonderful brews of Trafalgar.

Trafalgar Ales and Meads.
1156 Speers Road
Oakville, ON
905-337-0133
www.alesandmeads.com

Mike Arnold, President
Nancy Arnold, Co-Founder
George Hengstman, Co-Founder
Dave Jamieson, Head Brew master.
Lindsay Key, Marketing Director
Vince Maarsman, Cellar Man

TASTING NOTES

Harbour Gold 5%

Brewed in the tradition of pilsner-style lagers from the north of Europe, this light golden beer has a delicate hop aroma and subtle maltiness. It is an excellent compliment to white fish, veal, chicken and pork.

Harbour Light 4%

Although slightly lower in alcohol content than Harbour Gold, this light lager retains much of the delicate hopping and exquisite flavour of its big brother. Delicate fish and light pastas compliment.

Portside Amber 5%

This fine amber coloured ale uses a unique selection of different specialty malts and grains to develop a well-balanced counter to its aromatic hop finish. Hearty stews and red meats go well with this fine ale.

Paddy's Irish Red 5%

No colouring agents or artificial additives are used in this ancient Lett family recipe. The robust amber colour comes from the judicial use of crystal and carastan malts.

Celtic 4.5%

The Celtic formulation is based on an ancient recipe for Irish brown ale. Four different malts emphasize the grainy richness of this well-balanced ale. The flavour profile of Celtic is that of an easy-drinking, subtle ale with mild hopping.

Red Hill Mild 2.9%

Mild ales were the backbone of nourishment for the English working class prior to the turn of the last century. Trafalgar's Mild demonstrates that a light beer can be rich in malt flavour while being low in alcohol. This excellent, all-day summer ale is a compliment to vegetable dishes and darker poultry such as turkey or duck.

Elora ESB 5%

Brewed in the tradition of the finest English Pale Ales, Extra Special Bitter is a delight to ale connoisseurs. Fuggles hops provide this ale with noticeable hop bitterness. Great with fish dishes and lighter meals.

Elora Grand Lager 4%

Imported Saaz hops contribute a delicate aroma to this delightful beer. Light in colour, yet complex in flavour, Grand Lager was developed to be the perfect beer for a warm summer day, and it is great with spicy foods.

Elora Irish Ale 5%

Irish ales are dark and rich in colour, but are smooth and developed as an every day beer. A complex blend of imported hops and roasted barley give this ale a light aroma and a bittersweet finish.

SEASONAL

Downrigger Bock 6.5%

A dark, rich, and hearty German lager with a delightful bouquet and subtle sweetness. Available in the winter and late spring, our Bock is best enjoyed accompanied by rich foods such as duck, salmon, and game foods.

Granary Wheat 4.5%

Malted wheat and barley lend this ale a light aroma with a hint of citrus, giving it a creamy and refreshing palate. Granary Wheat is presented in filtered or North American fashion. A light hopping makes this a refreshing summer beer.

Abbey Belgian 6.5%

The flavour of Belgian style ales is unique in the world of beer. Trafalgar's version runs to rich and spicy with citrus notes and complex flavours. As dictated by the style, the hop bouquet is very subtle. The higher alcohol content results in a gentle sweetness that lends itself to after dinner sipping with desserts and fine chocolate.

MEADS

Raspberry, Blueberry, Black Currant, Tropical, Citrus, and **Wildberry** flavours. Semi-dry and slightly carbonated. A truly refreshing and unique beverage.

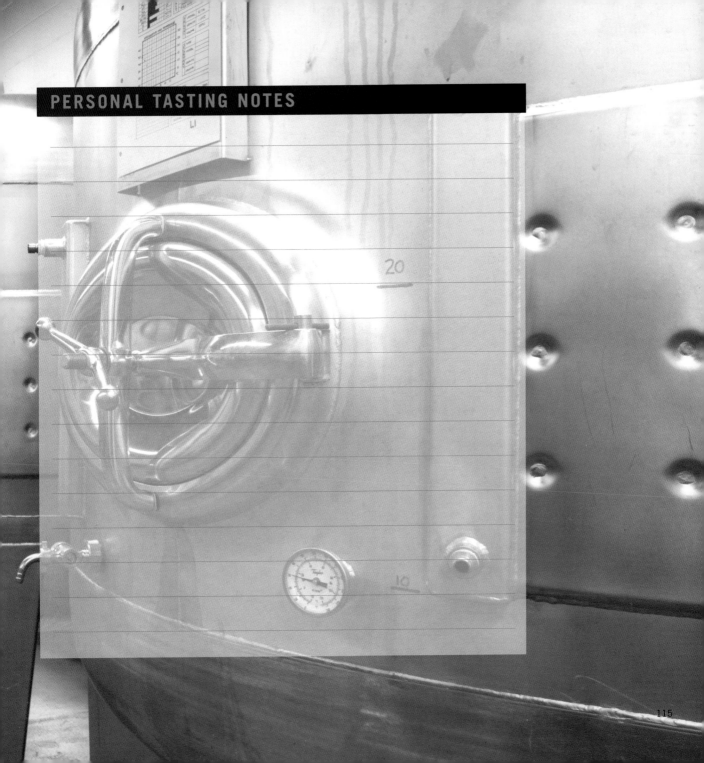

WALKERVILLE BREWING Co.

*W*alkerville is steeped in brewing and distilling history. American Hiram Walker built a distillery in this town back in 1854, hence the town's name. Soon after, Walker also established the Walkerville Brewery, which became one of the largest in Ontario. Its beers were popular all over North America, but it closed its doors in 1952. In 1998, Karen Behune Plunkett obtained the right to use the name, and she set about creating a new craft brewery with all the tradition and excellence of the previous one. Karen even set up her new brewery in an old Hiram Walker whisky warehouse, adding to the nostalgic charm of the newly reborn Walkerville Brewing Company. With over 25 years experience in the restaurant business, the brewery was an extension of Karen and her husband Michael's considerable talents. Karen wanted Walkerville to be a part

Brewmaster Jason Britton

of the community, offering a quality product locally brewed, and she has marvelously succeeded at both tasks.

The first beer from the brewery was a classic amber lager, and with its full-bodied crisp taste, it soon became a huge favourite in local bars and restaurants. Next was a Belgian-style premium blonde—perfect for hot summer days on local patios. The most recent addition to Walkerville's award winning brews is a new superior light beer, and its lower alcohol content takes nothing away from the taste of this full-bodied beer. Such

is the excellence in brewing at Walkerville that all three beers won gold medals at the 2004 Canadian Brewing Awards, and the brewery picked up the coveted Brewery of the Year award that year as well.

The local Windsor area had known and enjoyed Walkerville beers for a few years, but with the awards the word spread quickly across Ontario. Many fine bars and restaurants now feature its beers, including Café Volo and the Jamie Kennedy Wine Bar, both in Toronto. Walkerville is also available at selected Beer Stores and LCBO's. Of course,

if one wants to visit the brewery, there is a retail store on site where you can purchase bottles or the party-sized Growler—a "moonshine jug" that is equivalent to a six-pack.

Karen is a tireless worker when it comes to promoting her brewery. It's her passion, and it is also in her blood as her ancestors were the first "malters" in Ireland, supplying malt to the Guinness brewery at St. James Gate in Dublin. Today, her brew master Jason Britton brews small batches using only the best ingredients with no additives or preservatives to ensure that Walkerville beers are of the highest quality and freshness. Karen's background in the restaurant business has also helped her develop some great food recipes using her beers, such as beer mussels, beer braised baby back ribs, and fish tacos in beer batter. For these and more recipes check out the brewery's website. The brewery also has a beer trailer that one can hire for events, and with a capacity to hold 50 kegs, it's sure to be a big hit at any function. Walkerville Brewery is a great tradition brought back to life by the hard work and determination of Karen and her team—a tradition that looks to stand the test of time.

President and co-founder
Karen Behune Plunkett

TASTING NOTES

Classic Amber
Bright amber colour with a creamy white head releasing subtle noble hop aromas, and a slightly toasty malt flavour up front that gives way to a firm hop flavour. A wonderfully balanced finish that is long and refreshingly dry. Full bodied, spicy, and crisp.

Premium Blonde
The recipe is based on a Belgian style "blond" beer, born from the cellar slowly.

Softer in flavour, golden in colour, and a smooth but subtle hop flavour. A well-rounded beer for easy consumption.

Superior Light
Without sacrificing flavour, this all-natural light pilsner embodies the characteristics of traditional European brewing techniques and ingredients. Superior Light delivers 3.9% alcohol volume, reduced carbohydrates, and lower calories.

When in the Walkerville area you can also enjoy a part of history and a great pint of Walkerville at the nearby Kildare House. This house once belonged to the Hiram Walker distillery doctor and is a fascinating little pub.

Walkerville Brewing Company
525 Argyle Road
Windsor, ON N8Y 4Z8
519-255-9192
www.walkervillebrew.com

Karen Behune Plunkett, President
Jason Britton, Brew Master

WELLINGTON COUNTY BREWERY

"*Try* A Welly On" is the slogan for the Wellington Brewery, the oldest independent microbrewery in Canada. Of course, the "Welly" is the rubber boot named after the Duke of Wellington, but it's also the cleverly-designed tap handle for the brewery's draught taps. This unique-shaped handle has to be the most recognized and original in the craft brewing business. Founded back in 1985, Wellington celebrated its 20th anniversary in September of 2005 with a huge bash at the brewery. Brew master Mike Stirrup has been there from day one, first as an assistant, and eventually taking over as president in 2000. Back in the early days, owner Philip Gosling was instrumental in mapping out the Bruce Trail, and Wellington brews Trailhead Lager in his honour. Mike has trained with the best, both here and in England, including with Alan Griffiths, a brew master with a passion for true bitters. The brewery produces Arkell Best Bitter, available in cask, and as true a pint of bitter as you will find in Ontario. The Wellington County Ale is also available in cask and is another huge favourite with real ale drinkers.

Founder and brewmaster Mike Stirrup

During the construction of the brewery back in the mid-80's, the ship transporting the Hickley of London brewing equipment for Wellington was diverted to assist in the Air India disaster. The perfectionists at Wellington insisted that in order to brew traditional English Ales, even the equipment had to be English, so they delayed the opening until the equipment was finally shipped to them. The delay was well worth the wait as the brews have been winning awards ever since. The real cask ales of Wellington can be enjoyed from Windsor to Ottawa, and enthusiasts will go that bit further to have hand pumped beers served in the traditional way. The brewery is a proud member of Campaign for Real Ale (CAMRA) based in the U.K.

Trailhead lager is also getting rave reviews and was voted the number one lager in the 2005 Ontario Brewing Awards. It beat out many more established brands and identified Wellington as not only brewers of fine ales, but of lagers also. The Imperial Stout also came first place in the best stout category. This great beer is not for the timid—with an alcohol level of 8%, it has a wonderful depth and complexity and an almost coffee-like flavour.

The brewery puts its success down to time-honoured traditional beers brewed in small batches using all natural ingredients and a lot of patience. There is a wealth of experience at Wellington and a passion shared by all who work there. For instance, Mike Stirrup and Doug Dawkins have been at the brewery for a combined total of 35 years.

Wellington was one of the earliest craft breweries in Ontario, and its products can

now be found province-wide in over 650 bars and restaurants, as well as most Beer Stores and LCBOs. The brewery in Guelph employs ten full-time workers and ten part-time as demand for its beers continues to grow (and indeed it grew a whopping 50% over the last year). The large hospitality room within the brewery is the Iron Duke House, which has the feel and look of a large cozy pub with its large Oak bar, wooden beams, and roaring fire. The Iron Duke is often used for licensee training, and is a wonderful end to a brewery tour, as beer enthusiasts get to taste the great ales and lagers. There is also a retail beer and gift store on site where you can buy tee-shirts and caps displaying the "Welly" boot. Being established in the community for 20 years, the brewery is proudly associated with a host of local charities including The Big Brothers Assocation and the Guelph Wish Fund for Children.

Wellington sponsors many fundraising events to help these and other causes. Wellington ales were also the official beer of the Johnny Cash biopic *Walk The Line*

For a pint of Wellington in the area try these fine pubs: the Woolwich Arms and the Shakespeare Arms in Guelph, the Duke of Wellington in Waterloo, and the Copper Kettle in Fergus. Just ask for a pint of "Welly."

Wellington Brewery
950 Woodlawn Road West
Guelph, ON N1K 1B8
519-837-2337
www.wellingtonbrewery.ca

Michael Stirrup, President and Brew Master
Doug Dawkins, Vice-President and Brewery Manager

TASTING NOTES

Arkell Beat Bitter 4%
A refreshing beer described as the most flavourful light beer in Ontario. Also available as cask conditioned real ale.

County Ale 5%
A full bodied traditional ale, matured slowly for smoothness and balance. Also available as cask conditioned real ale.

Special Pale Ale 4.5%
A refreshing and creamy smooth ale that is notably full of flavour. A summertime patio beer.

Beehive Honey Lager 5.2%
A hint of wild Ontario honey flavours this refreshing, pale gold lager.

Trailhead Lager 4.5%
A Euro-traditional style award winning lager derived from Czech hops. Crisp and refreshing.

Iron Duke Strong Ale 6.5%
A connoisseurs delight, a dark ale with a malty, nutty complexity and layers of flavour.

Imperial Stout 8%
A rich, dark beer of exceptional depth and complexity with an almost coffee like flavour.

PERSONAL TASTING NOTES